FIRST TIME LEARNING

NUMBERS

Here's a short note for parents:

We recommend that you work through this book with your child, offering guidance and encouragement along the way.

Find a quiet place to sit, preferably at a table, and encourage your child to hold their pencil correctly.

Try to work at your child's pace and avoid spending too long on any one page or activity.

Most of all, emphasize the fun element of what you are doing and enjoy yourselves. Don't forget to use your stickers!

AUTUMN
PUBLISHING

1
2
3
4
5
6
7
8
9
10

Know your numbers!

Find the missing cake sticker.

Count the candles on each cake, saying the numbers out loud.

Place your sticker here

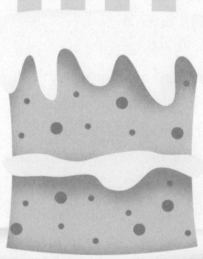

How old are you? Can you find that number of candles?

Place your reward sticker here

Birthday candles

Count the candles and draw a circle around the right numbers.

1 2 3

1 2 3 4

1 2 3 4 5

Birthday presents

Find a sticker of some presents.

Count the presents. Say the numbers out loud as you count.

Place your sticker here

Place your reward sticker here

More numbers

Find a sticker with two ducks.

Count the ducks and say the numbers.

Place your sticker here

Can you count from 1–10, then count all
the way back again?

Place your
reward sticker
here

Quack, quack

Count the ducks and circle the right numbers.

6 7 8 9 10

6 7 8 9 10

Frog march

Find a sticker with two frogs.

Count the frogs. Say the numbers out loud as you count.

Place your
sticker here

Place your
reward sticker
here

Number rhymes

Here are two number rhymes to sing.

1, 2, 3, 4, 5 once I caught a fish alive

1, 2, 3, 4, 5 once I caught a fish alive,
6, 7, 8, 9, 10 then I let it go again.
Why did you let it go?
Because it bit my finger so.
Which finger did it bite?
This little finger on the right!

1
2
3
4
5
6
7
8
9
10

Place your
sticker here

Place your
reward sticker
here

Find a fish sticker.

Count the fish in the picture and color them in.

Sizzling sausages

Five fat sausages sizzling in a pan,
All of a sudden **one** went bang!
Four fat sausages sizzling in a pan,
All of a sudden **one** went bang!
Three fat sausages sizzling in a pan,
All of a sudden **one** went bang!
Two fat sausages sizzling in a pan,
All of a sudden **one** went bang!
One fat sausage sizzling in a pan,
All of a sudden **one** went bang!
Now there are no fat sausages sizzling in the pan!

Place your
sticker here

Find a sausage sticker.

Count the sausages in the picture and color them in.

Place your
reward sticker
here

1
2
3
4
5
6
7
8
9
10

Write 1, 2, 3, 4, 5

Numbers big and numbers small.
Can you count and write them all?

Count the dots. Say the numbers. Write the numbers.

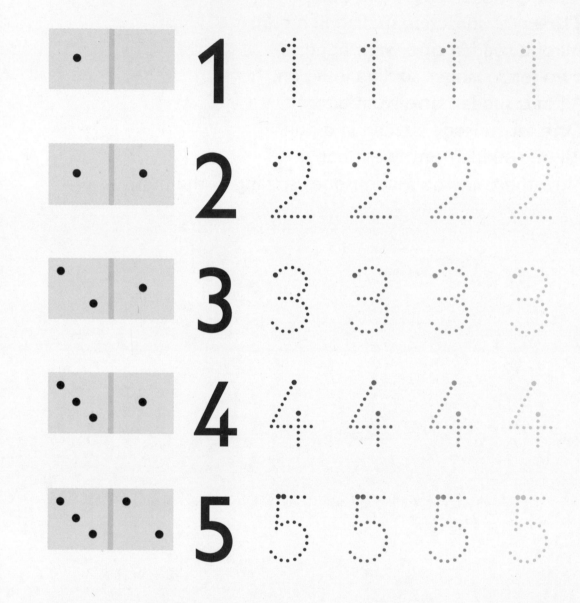

Dotty dog

Find a dotty dog sticker.

How many dots are there
on the dog?

Place your
sticker here

Place your
reward sticker
here

5   dots

Write 6, 7, 8, 9, 10

Count the dots. Say the numbers. Write the numbers.

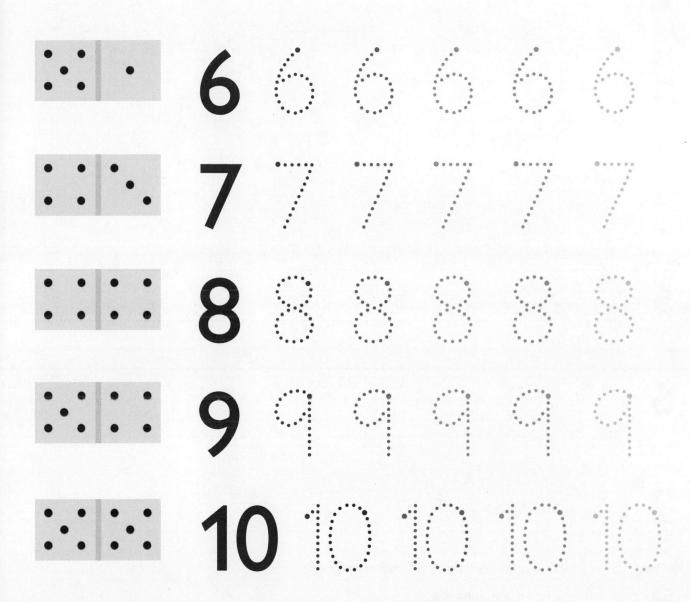

6   6   6   6   6   6

7   7   7   7   7   7

8   8   8   8   8   8

9   9   9   9   9   9

10   10   10   10   10

Spotty pig

Find a spotty pig sticker.

How many spots are there

on the pig?

10   spots

Place your sticker here

Place your reward sticker here

1
2
3
4
5
6
7
8
9
10

Keep your toys tidy
Find the pencil sticker.
Now count all the toys.

Place your
sticker here

How many are there of each type of toy?
Trace the numbers in the boxes.

4	7	3
balls	cars	dinosaurs

6	4
pencils	trains

Place your
reward sticker
here

Paintbrushes and paint pots

Count the paintbrushes and trace the numbers in the boxes.

Counting toys

Count each group of toys. Draw a line between each group and the matching number.

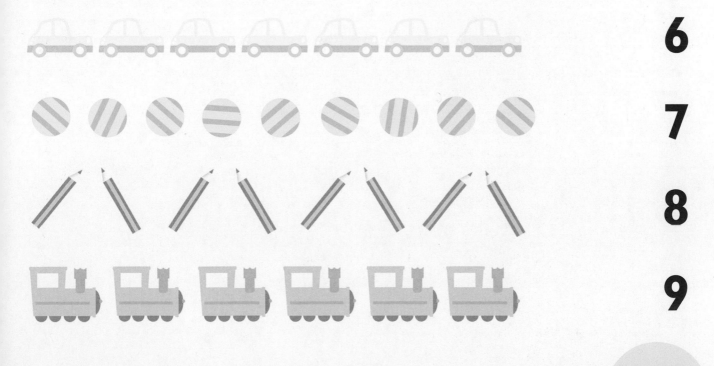

6

7

8

9

Color the most
Color the tree with the most birds.

Find a bird sticker.
Color the bird with the most tail feathers.

Place your
sticker here

What's missing?

Write the missing number on the egg in each line.

5　◯　7　8　9　10

◯　6　7　8　9　10

5　6　7　◯　9　10

Hoppity hop!

Count the hops the bird has made.

Find the number sticker that fits at the end of the row.

1　2　3　4　5　Place your sticker here

Count the hops and write the numbers.

1

Place your reward sticker here

1 2 3 4 5 6 7 8 9 10

One more

Count the treats. Then draw one more.
Write how many there are now.

popsicles

pieces of candy

ice cream cones

Candy counting

Count the candy in each bag.

Find the number stickers to label the candy bags.

Place your sticker here

Place your sticker here

Place your sticker here

Place your reward sticker here

Color the bag with the most pieces of candy.

One less

Cross out one thing in each line and write how many are left.

Cup counting

Count the drinks on each tray and write the numbers in the boxes.

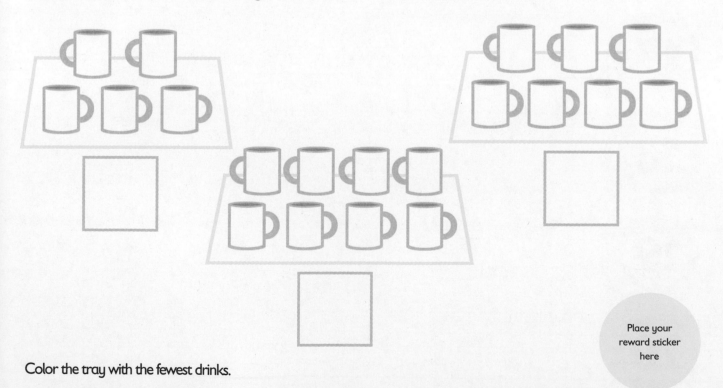

Color the tray with the fewest drinks.

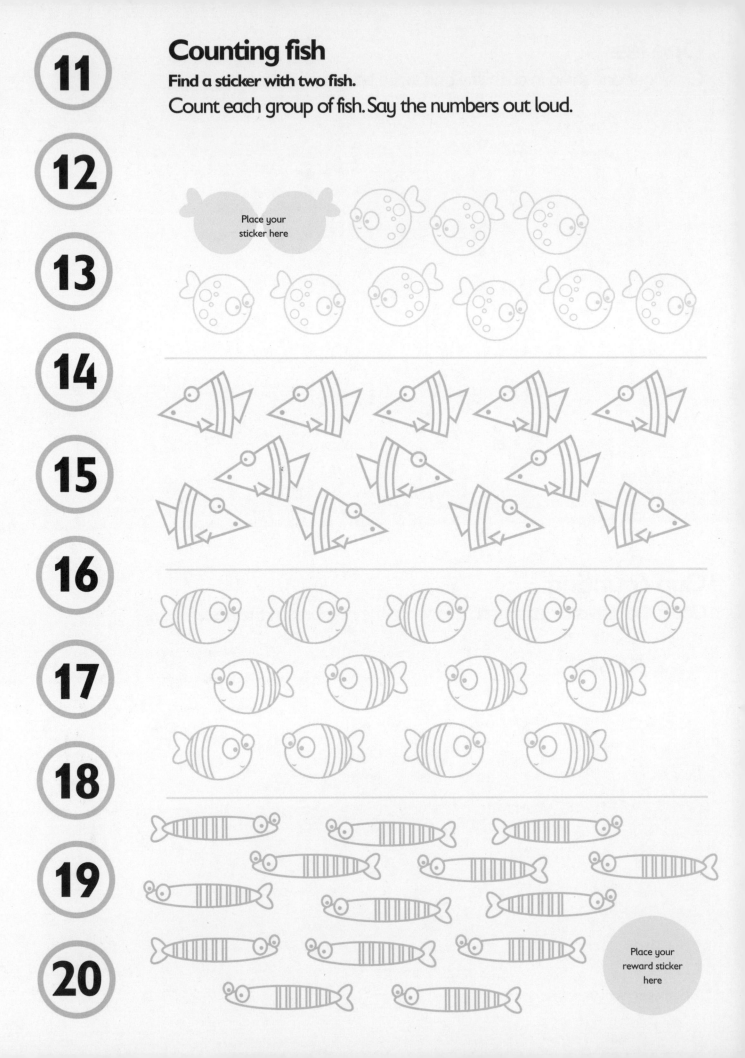

Counting fish

Find a sticker with two fish.

Count each group of fish. Say the numbers out loud.

Place your sticker here

Place your reward sticker here

Turtles

Count the turtles. Draw a circle around the number.

11 12 13 14 15

16 17 18 19 20

Starfish everywhere!

Count the starfish.

Find a sticker with more starfish.

Now count how many starfish there are all together.

Did you count **15** starfish?

Place your
sticker here

Place your
reward sticker
here

Write 11, 12, 13, 14, 15

Find a domino sticker.

Count the dots. Trace the numbers with a pencil.

Place your sticker here

11 11 11 11 11

12 12 12 12 12

13 13 13 13 13

14 14 14 14

15 15 15 15

Place your reward sticker here

Flower show

Count the flowers. Trace the numbers on the pots.

Seedlings to grow

Count each group of seeds. Draw lines to match the seeds to the packets.

❋ **12**

❋ **13**

❋ **14**

❋ **15**

Place your reward sticker here

Write 16, 17, 18, 19, 20

Count the dots. Trace the numbers with a pencil.

16 16 16 16 16

17 17 17 17 17

18 18 18 18 18

19 19 19 19 19

20 20 20 20 20

Place your reward sticker here

What's missing?

Write the missing number on the leaf in each line.

Hoppity hop!

Count the hops the frog has made.

Find the number sticker that fits at the end of the row.

Two by two

Find the missing sticker.

Draw lines to match each pair of animals.

How many animal pairs are there all together?

Say the number out loud.

Place your sticker here

Place your reward sticker here

Two more

Draw **two** more items in each line. Count the cars and the cones.
Write the numbers in the boxes.

cars

cones

Two less

Cross out **two** things in each line. Count the things left in each line.
Write the number in the box.

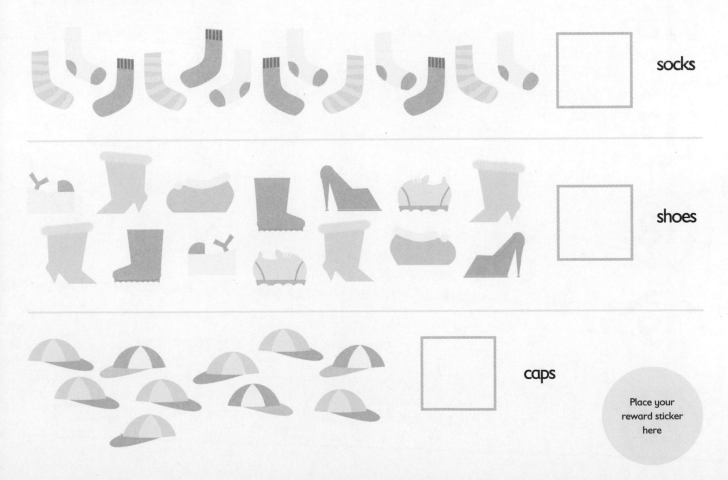

socks

shoes

caps

Hide-and-seek numbers
Numbers here, numbers there, numbers hiding everywhere!

The numbers **1** to **20** are in this picture.

Can you find them all? Color in the picture.

Place your reward sticker here

1
2
3
4
5
6
7
8
9
10

Numbers everywhere

Number **one**, number **two**,
is there a number on your shoe?
Number **three**, number **four**,
what's the number on your door?

Look around you. Can you see any numbers?
Write the numbers on the line.

… … … … … … … … … … … … … … … … … … … …

… … … … … … … … … … … … … … … … … … … …

What's your shoe size? … … … … … … … … … … … … … … …

… … … … … … … … …

What's your house number? … … … … … … … … … … … … … …

**Find the missing number sticker
for the phone.**

Write your phone number here:

… … … … … … … … … … … … … …

… … … … … … … … … … …

Place your
sticker here

Place your
reward sticker
here

Tick-tock

Numbers tell us what time it is.

Find the missing number sticker for the clock.

What time is it?

Place your sticker here

Place your reward sticker here

Happy birthday to you!

Numbers tell you when it is your birthday.

Find the missing number sticker.

Find the day of your birthday on this calendar.

Color in the square. How old are you now?

How old will you be on your next birthday?

1	2	3	4	5
6	7	8	9	10
11	12	13	14	15
16	17	18	Place your sticker here	20
21	22	23	24	25
26	27	28	29	30
31				

Place your reward sticker here

Money

Look at these coins.

Can you draw them in order in the circles?

Start with the coin worth the smallest amount.

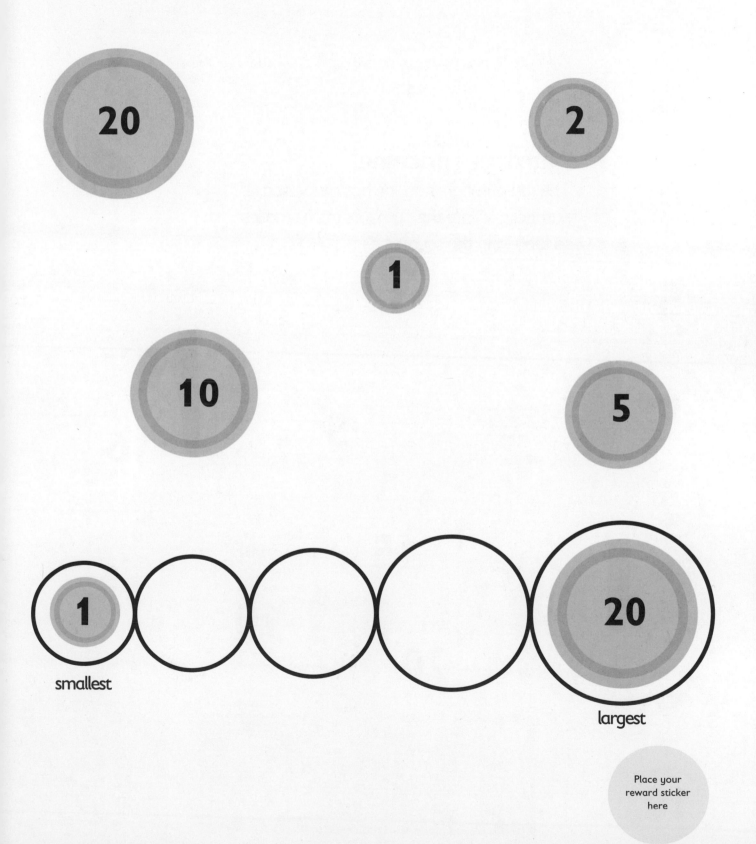

smallest

largest

Big and small numbers

Numbers big and numbers small,
show me that you know them all!

What's the **smallest** number you know? … … … … … … … … … … … …
… … … ..

What's the **largest** number you know? … … … … … … … … … … … .
… … … .

What's your favorite number? … … … … … … … … … … … … … …

Number machine

The fun number machine has made some
numbers. Write the numbers from smallest
to largest in the squares.

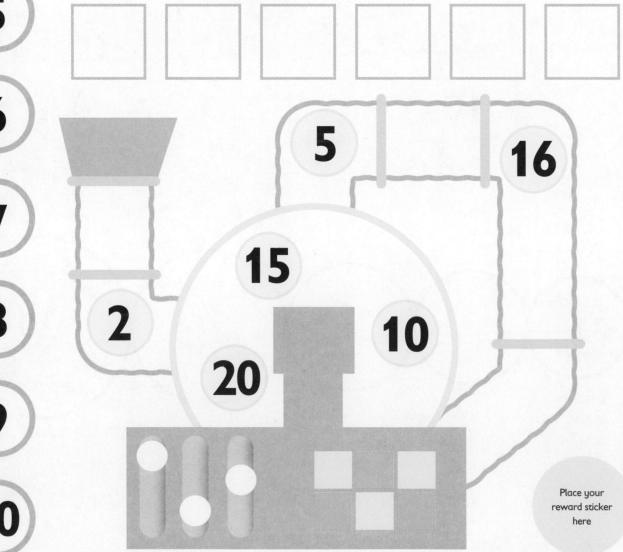

Place your
reward sticker
here

Millions and billions!

These are huge, enormous, gigantic numbers.
They are bigger than you can count.

Just imagine the millions of stars that are in the sky!

Find a sticker with a huge, enormous, gigantic number.

Place your
sticker here

Place your
reward sticker
here

This is how we write **one million**.

Connect the dots

Start at number **1** and join the numbered dots in order.

How many dots are there?

Well done! You're a star for finishing this section!

FIRST TIME LEARNING

EARLY MATH

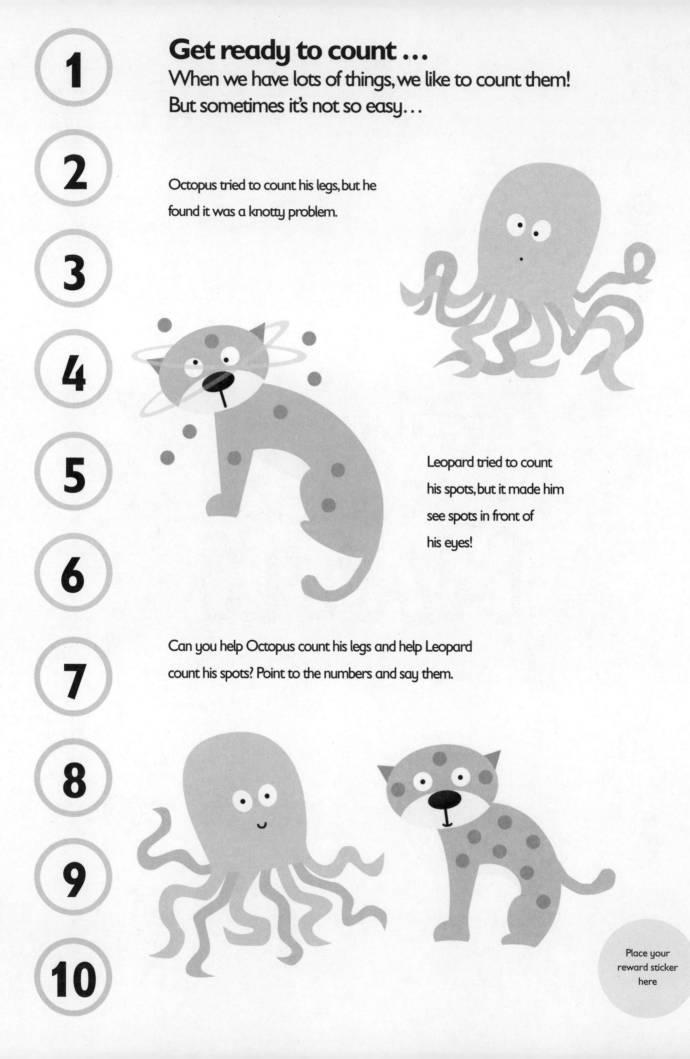

Get ready to count …

When we have lots of things, we like to count them!
But sometimes it's not so easy…

Octopus tried to count his legs, but he found it was a knotty problem.

Leopard tried to count his spots, but it made him see spots in front of his eyes!

Can you help Octopus count his legs and help Leopard count his spots? Point to the numbers and say them.

1
2
3
4
5
6
7
8
9
10

Place your reward sticker here

Buckle my shoe

Find a door sticker.
There are rhymes to help Octopus and Leopard learn to count.
Here's one of them.

1, 2, buckle my shoe.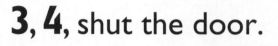

3, 4, shut the door.

Place your
sticker here

5, 6, pick up sticks.

7, 8, lay them straight.

9, 10, a speckled hen.

Place your
reward sticker
here

How many eggs has the speckled hen laid?

What can you see?

What can you see when you count with me?

Find a bee sticker and a star sticker.

Count up to **3** birds in the tree.

Count up to **5** bees in the hive.

Place your sticker here

Count up to **7** stars in heaven.

Place your sticker here

Count up to **9** clothes on the line.

Count **10** or more shells on the shore.

How many shells on the shore?

Were there more than **10**?

Place your reward sticker here

Crazy creatures

How many animals are there?

Count each line of animals and circle the correct number.

1 2 3 4 5 6 7 8 9 10

1 2 3 4 5 6 7 8 9 10

1 2 3 4 5 6 7 8 9 10

1 2 3 4 5 6 7 8 9 10

Place your reward sticker here

How many legs?

How many legs do you have?

Find a spider sticker.

Count the legs and write the numbers in the boxes.
Which animal has the most legs? Which has the fewest legs?
Do any animals have the same number of legs?

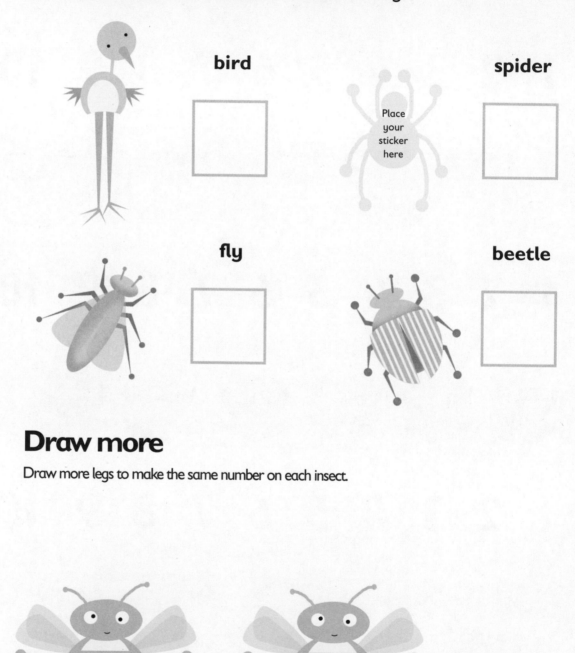

bird

spider

Place your sticker here

fly

beetle

Draw more

Draw more legs to make the same number on each insect.

Place your reward sticker here

Counting down

Write the missing numbers for the countdown from **10** to **1**.

10

9

7

6

4

3

1

BLAST OFF!

Place your reward sticker here

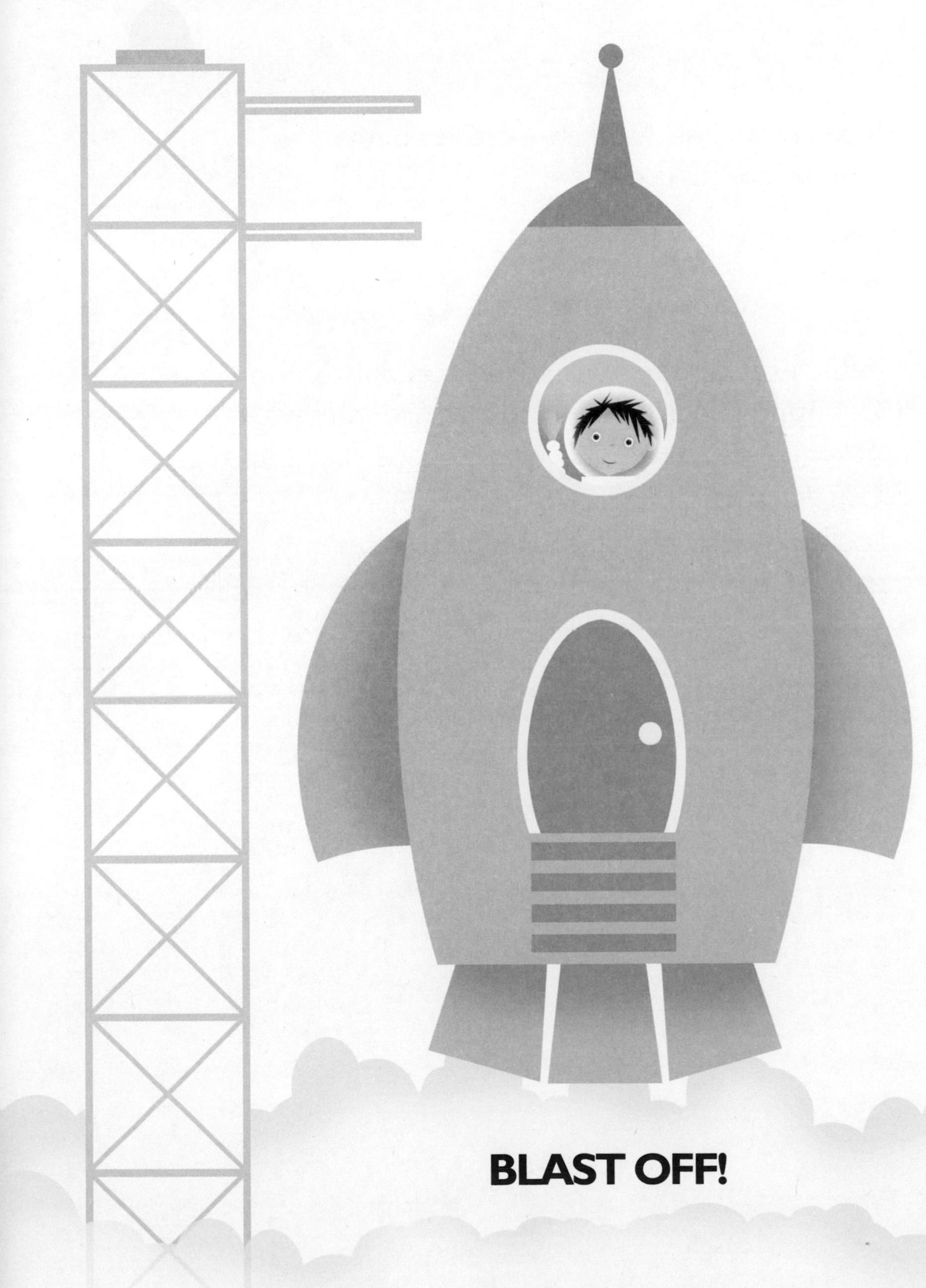

Look again!

Here are some dots. Can you count them?

Now count these. Are there more, less or the same number as above?

Which set of dots was easier to count? Counting is easier when things are in rows.

Look and guess

Look at each set of shapes. Guess the number in each set, then count them.

Number patterns

Find a diamond sticker.

Copy each pattern, then guess the number of shapes you have drawn.
Write the number in the box.

Doodle drawings

Draw a house. Color it in using **3** colors.

Now draw another picture of a house.
This time color it in using **5** colors.

Find a sticker of a very colorful house.
Count all the colors you see on the house.
Write the number of colors
in the box below.

Place your
sticker here

Place your
reward sticker
here

1
2
3
4
5
6
7
8
9
10

Birds of a feather

Look at these birds. Answer the counting questions.

Find a bird sticker.

Place your
sticker here

How many birds ...

... have thin tails?   ... have curly tails?

... have short tails?   ... have bushy tails?

Place your
reward sticker
here

Looking at shapes

Can you make a circle shape with your hands and fingers? Can you make a triangle shape?

Here are some names for different shapes.

square

circle

triangle

rectangle

Shapes all around

Find a sticker of a plate. What shape is it?

Draw a line to connect the plate to the matching shape.

Place your
sticker here

Find a sticker of a window. What shape is it?

Draw a line to connect the window to the matching shape.

Place your
sticker here

Place your
reward sticker
here

1
2
3
4
5
6
7
8
9
10

Robot shapes

Find a sticker of a robot's head.

Can you see the shapes that make up the robot?

Place your sticker here

Count the shapes in the robot picture.

Write how many of each shape there are in the boxes below.

Find the missing shape stickers.

Place your sticker here

Place your sticker here

Place your sticker here

Place your sticker here

Place your reward sticker here

1
2
3
4
5
6
7
8
9
10

Sorting shapes

Round shapes here, square shapes there.
There are shapes everywhere!

Color the shapes with **4** sides yellow.

Color the shapes with **3** sides blue.

Color the other shapes red.

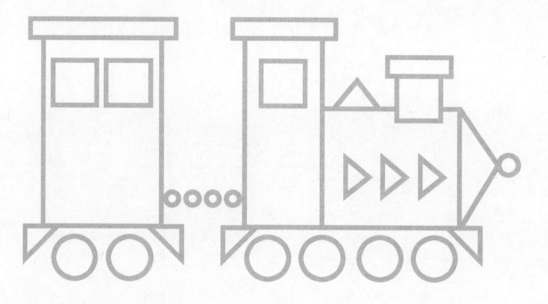

How many shapes are there?

yellow
shapes

blue
shapes

red
shapes

Place your
sticker here

Find a sticker of a kite.

How many triangles are there on the kite?

Place your
reward sticker
here

Terrible twins

Draw the missing shapes to make the robots the same.

Matching shapes

Color the two shapes in each line that are exactly the same.

Patterns

We can put shapes and numbers in a row to make patterns.

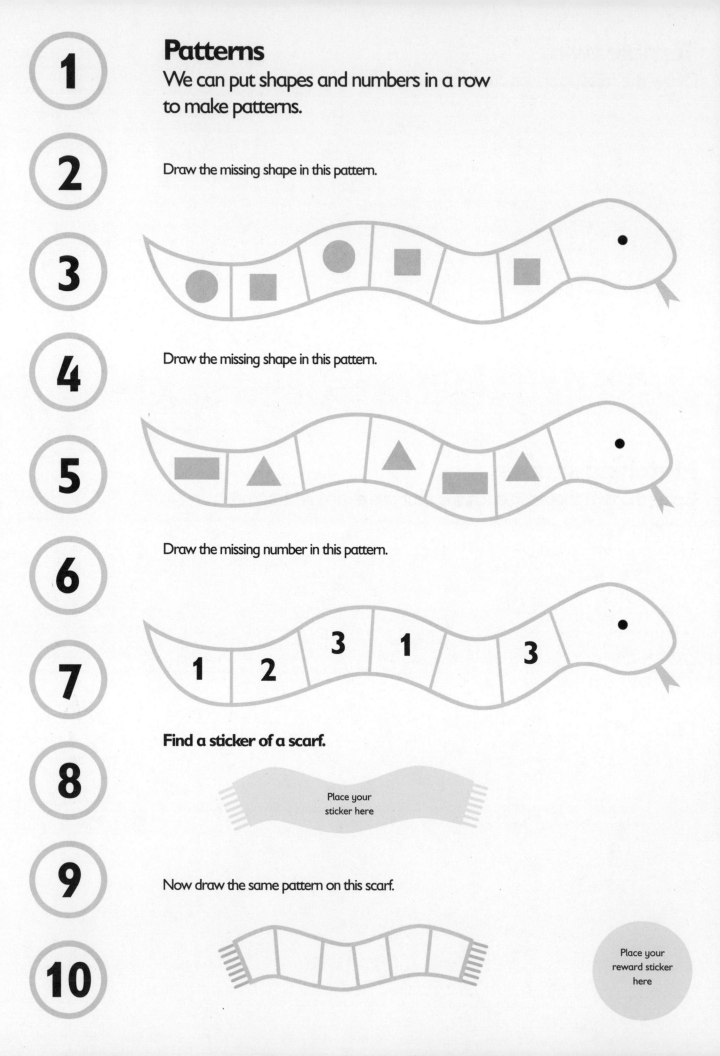

Draw the missing shape in this pattern.

Draw the missing shape in this pattern.

Draw the missing number in this pattern.

Find a sticker of a scarf.

Place your sticker here

Now draw the same pattern on this scarf.

The same on both sides

Color the butterfly's wings so that they are the same on both sides.

How many eyes does the butterfly have?

Finish the pictures

Trace the dotted lines to finish these shapes.

1

2

3

4

5

6

7

8

9

10

What size?
When we want to know the size of something, we measure it.

Find a sticker of a tree.

Which is the tallest tree? Color it in.

Place your sticker here

Which is the longest log? Color it in.

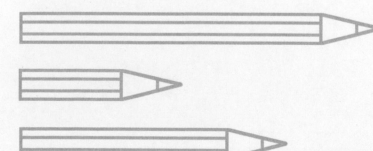

Smallest and shortest
Color the smallest shoe.

Color the shortest pencil.

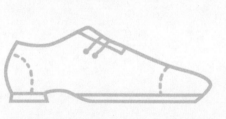

Place your reward sticker here

Fitting in

Find a sticker of a cereal box.

How many cereal boxes can fit in the cabinets?

Draw them.

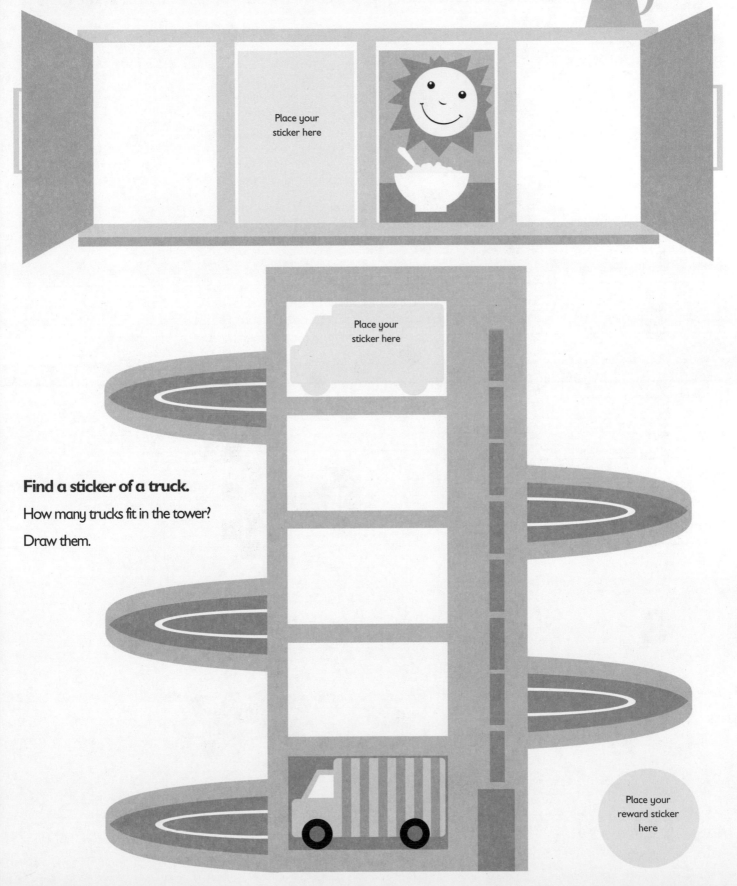

Place your sticker here

Find a sticker of a truck.

How many trucks fit in the tower?

Draw them.

Place your sticker here

Place your reward sticker here

First and last

Find the sticker of the flag to finish the picture.

In this story what picture comes first, what picture comes in the middle and what picture comes last? Write **1**, **2** and **3** in the boxes.

START

FINISH

Place your sticker here

Place your reward sticker here

Long time or short time?

Find an ice cream sticker.

How long does it take to do each of these things?
Which things take a short time to do? Which take a long time?
Draw a line from each picture to the 'short time' or 'long time' box.

Watch your favorite
TV show.

Build a house.

Sing a song.

short time

Learn how
to be a doctor.

long time

Grow a tree
from a seed.

Fly around
the world.

Place
your
sticker
here

Eat an
ice cream.

Place your
reward sticker
here

Draw some more

How many things are in each row? Draw **1** more.

Write the new number in the box.

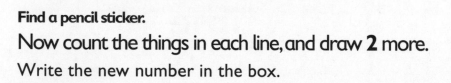

Find a pencil sticker.

Now count the things in each line, and draw **2** more.

Write the new number in the box.

Place your sticker here

Place your reward sticker here

1
2
3
4
5
6
7
8
9
10

Adding up

Here are some sums for you to try.
Count the pictures in each line and write the answer.

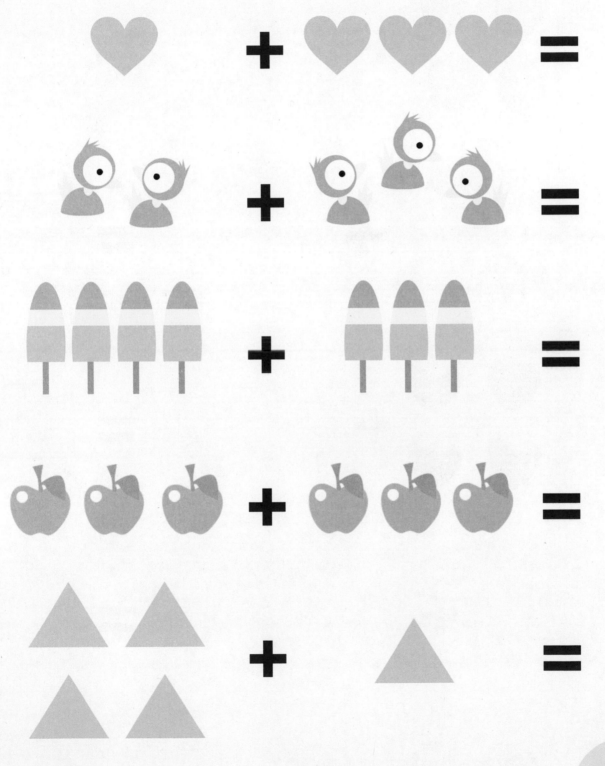

Place your
reward sticker
here

Double trouble

Find a snail sticker.

Count the things. Then draw the same number after the **+**. How many are there all together?

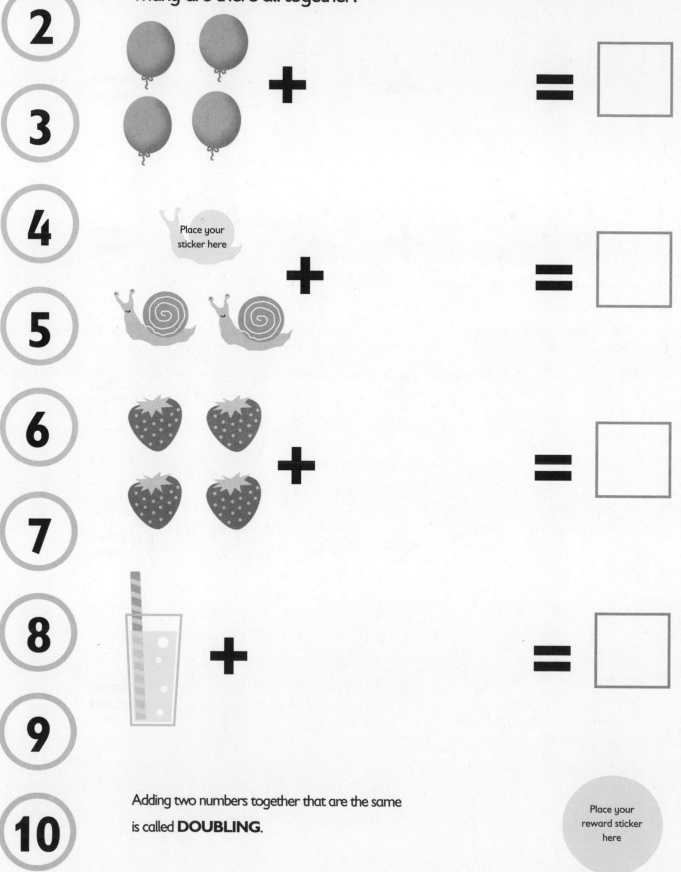

Adding two numbers together that are the same is called **DOUBLING**.

Place your reward sticker here

Making 5

How many are there all together? Write the answers in the boxes.

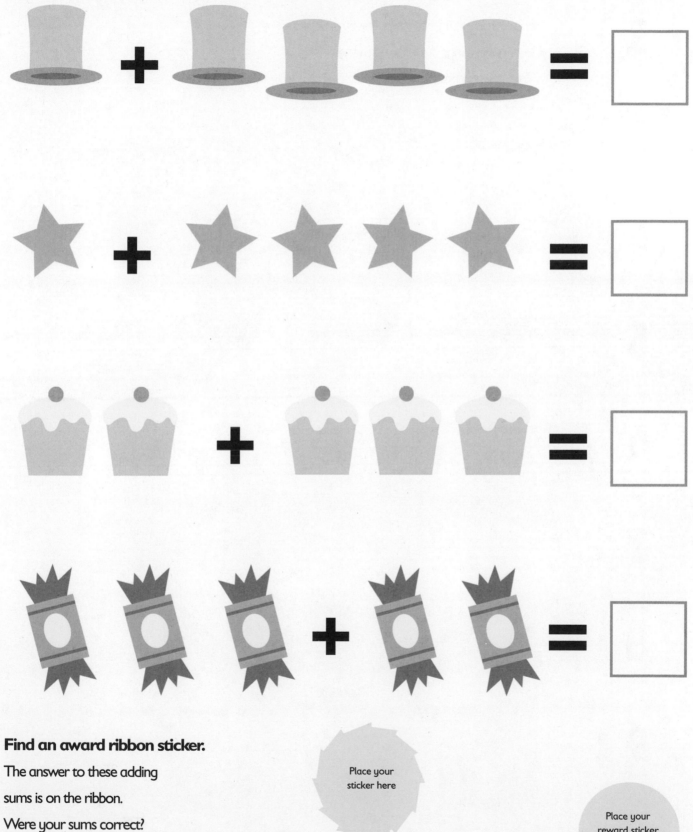

Find an award ribbon sticker.

The answer to these adding

sums is on the ribbon.

Were your sums correct?

Place your sticker here

Place your reward sticker here

Take away 1

Sometimes we want to make numbers less, so we take away.

Take away **1** thing from each line by crossing it out.

How many things are left in each line?

Write the number in the box.

Five teds in a bed

Find a teddy bear sticker.

This is a funny song. Can you learn it?

Place your sticker here

There were **5** in the bed and the little one said,
"Roll over, roll over."
So they all rolled over and one fell out.
There were **4** in the bed and the little one said,
"Roll over, roll over."
So they all rolled over and one fell out.
There were **3** in the bed and the little one said,
"Roll over, roll over."
So they all rolled over and one fell out.
There were **2** in the bed and the little one said,
"Roll over, roll over."
So they all rolled over and one fell out.
There was **1** in the bed and the little one said,
"Goodnight!"

Place your reward sticker here

1
2
3
4
5
6
7
8
9
10

Take away 2

Take away **2** things from each line by crossing them out. How many are left?

When we take away things using the ― sign,

the number gets less and we have less.

Find a sticker of 2 potted plants. Can you do the sum?

 ―  =

Place your
sticker here

Place your
reward sticker
here

Half and half

Count the objects in each line. Can you cross out **HALF** of them? Write how many are left in the box.

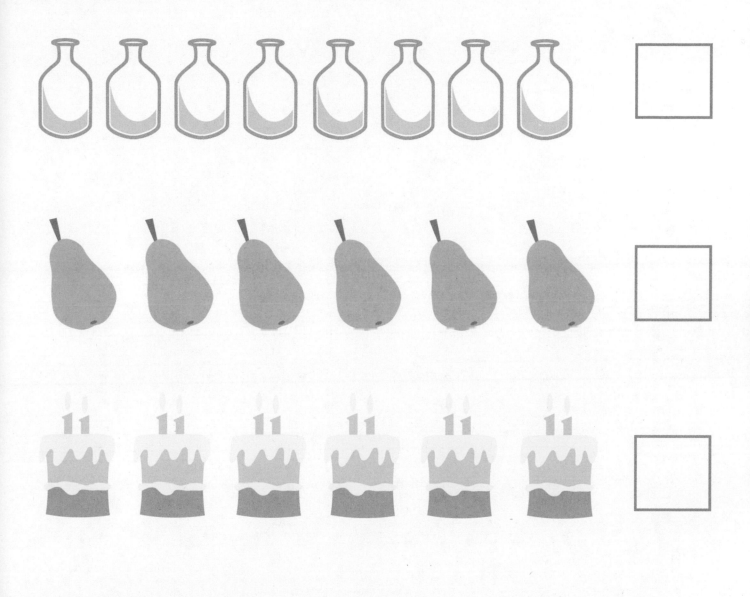

Sharing

Pass out the food for the animals.

Are there enough carrots for each rabbit to have **1** each?

Are there enough carrots for each rabbit to have **2** carrots?

Circle **2** carrots and draw a line to each rabbit.

Find a sticker of 8 leaves.

Place your sticker here

Place your reward sticker here

How many leaves can each caterpillar have?

Share the party food

There are **3** children at a party. They have **9** sausages, **6** cupcakes and **3** drinks between them. How many items does each child have? Write the answers.

drinks　　　　　**cupcakes**　　　　　**sausages**

Find a sticker of a sausage.

Place your sticker here

There were **10** sausages in the pack and the children ate **9**.

How many sausages were left?

Can you guess who ate the last sausage?

Place your reward sticker here

You're a star!

Find **5** triangles in the star. Color them yellow.

Find **1** pentagon in the star. Color it red.

Well done! You're a star for finishing this section!

Place your reward sticker here

FIRST TIME LEARNING
THE
ALPHABET

a
b
c
d
e
f
g
h
i
j
k
l
m

Pictures and letters

Here are the first five letters of the alphabet.

a b c d e

Here are some pictures. Point to each one and say the word. Find the sticker of the apple.

banana

apple

Place sticker here

cat

dog

elephant

Which letter starts each word?
Can you point to the letters and say them?

Place your reward sticker here

Find the matching pictures

Find the two matching pictures in each line and color them in.

Find the matching letters

Find the two matching letters in each line and circle them.

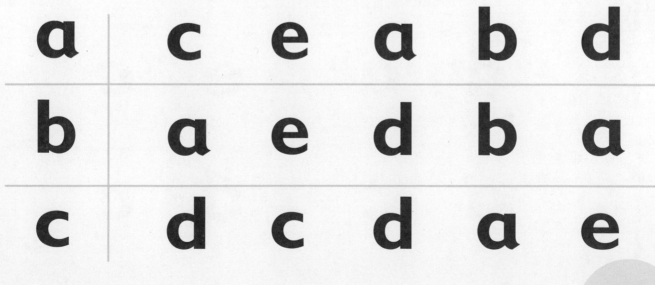

a
b
c
d
e
f
g
h
i
j
k
l
m

Make the pictures the same

Look at the pictures. Find a sticker to make the cats match. Add 6 spots to the dog to make them match.

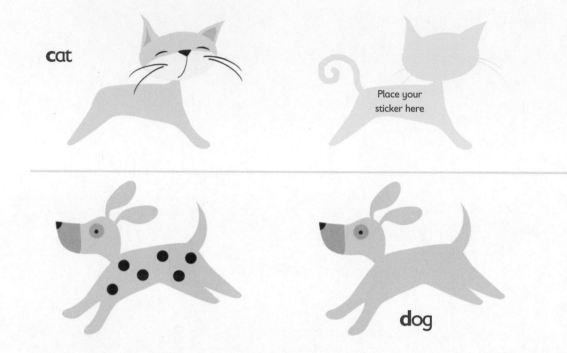

cat

Place your sticker here

dog

Make the letters the same

Look at these letters. Can you make the second letter look like the first letter?

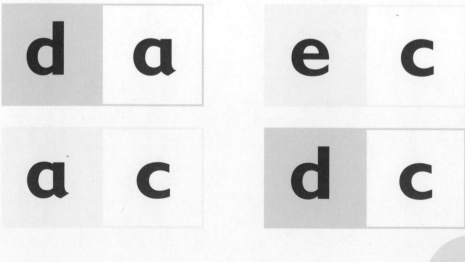

d a   e c

a c   d c

Place your reward sticker here

Odd one out

Find the odd one out in each line and circle it.

dog

dinosaur

Find the odd letter out in each line and circle it.

a a d a a

c c c e c

d d d d b

e a e e e

a
b
c
d
e
f
g
h
i
j
k
l
m

Let's get to know a, b, c

These things start with **a**.

apple   ant

Say the letter sound at the beginning of each word.

These things start with **b**.

ball   bed   bag

Can you think of other words that begin with
the **b** sound?

Place your
reward sticker
here

Now it's time for **c**. Point to the pictures and say the words.

car   cat   comb

Draw a line to join each picture to the first letter of its name.

a   b   c

a
b
c
d
e
f
g
h
i
j
k
l
m

Let's get to know d, e, f

Look at the pictures and say the words.

4 four

fish

elephant

duck

egg

dog

d   e   f

Draw lines to connect the pictures with the correct first letter.

Can you think of more things that begin with **d, e** or **f**?

Place your reward sticker here

Here's **d**. Can you find a sticker
of something that starts with **d**?

d

Place your
sticker here

Can you color the things that begin with **f**?

Place your
reward sticker
here

a
b
c
d
e
f
g
h
i
j
k
l
m

Let's get to know g, h, i

Look at the pictures and say the words.

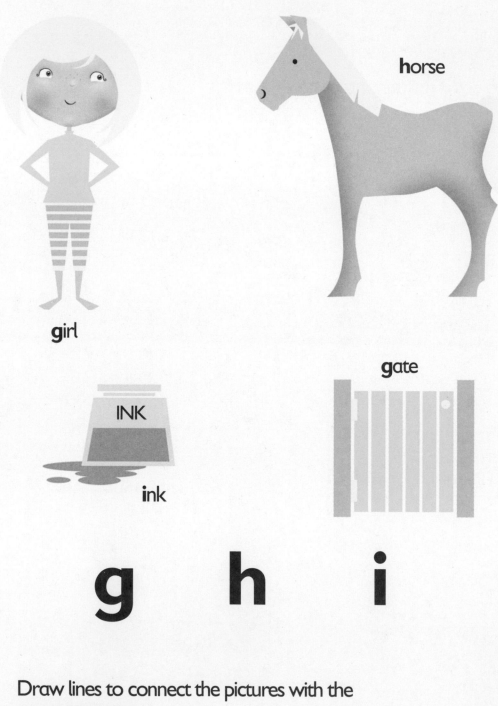

horse

girl

INK

ink

gate

g   h   i

Draw lines to connect the pictures with the correct first letter.

Do you know other words that begin with **g, h** or **i**?

Here's **g**. Can you find a
sticker of something that
starts with **g?**

Can you color the things that begin with **h?**

Let's get to know j, k, l

Look at the pictures and say the words.

kite

leaf

jam

key

jigsaw

j   k   l

Draw lines to connect the pictures with the correct first letter.

Circle **j** in each of these words.

jug   **jelly**   **jam**

jump   **jiggle**

Place your reward sticker here

Here's **k.** Can you find a sticker of something beginning with **k**?

k

What does little Lisa like? She only likes things that begin with the letter **l.** Only color the things that Lisa likes.

a
b
c
d
e
f
g
h
i
j
k
l
m

Seeing double

Draw lines to connect the letters that are the same.

f g h i j k

i k f g h j

Look at the pictures and say the words.

Trace the first letter in each word.

house helicopter

Can you find the letter **h** sticker?

Place your sticker here

Place your reward sticker here

Sort the shopping

Draw lines to put the items in the correct cart.

Find a sticker of something that begins with **b**. Put it in the cart.

n
o
p
q
r
s
t
u
v
w
x
y
z

Let's get to know m, n, o

Look at the pictures and say the words.

ostrich

nose

monster

octopus

m   n   o

Draw lines to connect the pictures with the correct first letter.

Here's **m**. Can you find a sticker of something beginning with **m**?

Place your sticker here

Place your reward sticker here

m

Here's **n**. Can you find a sticker that shows another **n**?

n

Color sounds

Can you find and color the one thing that begins with **o**?

n
o
p
q
r
s
t
u
v
w
x
y
z

Let's get to know p, q, r

Look at the pictures and say the words.

penguin

piano

quilt

ring

queen

p q r

Draw lines to connect the pictures with the correct first letter.

Place your reward sticker here

Here's **p.** Can you find
a sticter of something
beginning with **p**?

p

Place your
sticker here

Color the things that begin with **r**.

Place your
reward sticker
here

n
o
p
q
r
s
t
u
v
w
x
y
z

Let's get to know s, t, u

Look at the pictures and say the words.

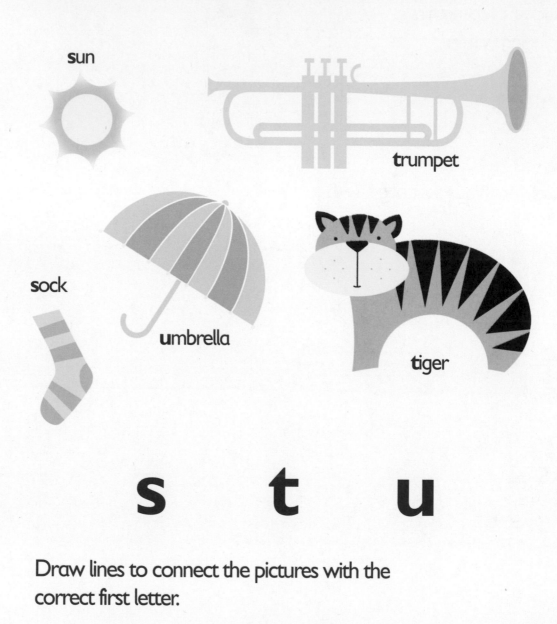

sun

trumpet

sock

umbrella

tiger

s   t   u

Draw lines to connect the pictures with the correct first letter.

Here's **s**. Can you find a sticker of something that begins with **s**?

Place your sticker here

Place your reward sticker here

s

Color the things that begin with **t**.

Circle **u** in each of these words.

sun   **us**   **fun**

nut   **bus**

n
o
p
q
r
s
t
u
v
w
x
y
z

Let's get to know v, w, x

Look at the pictures and say the words.

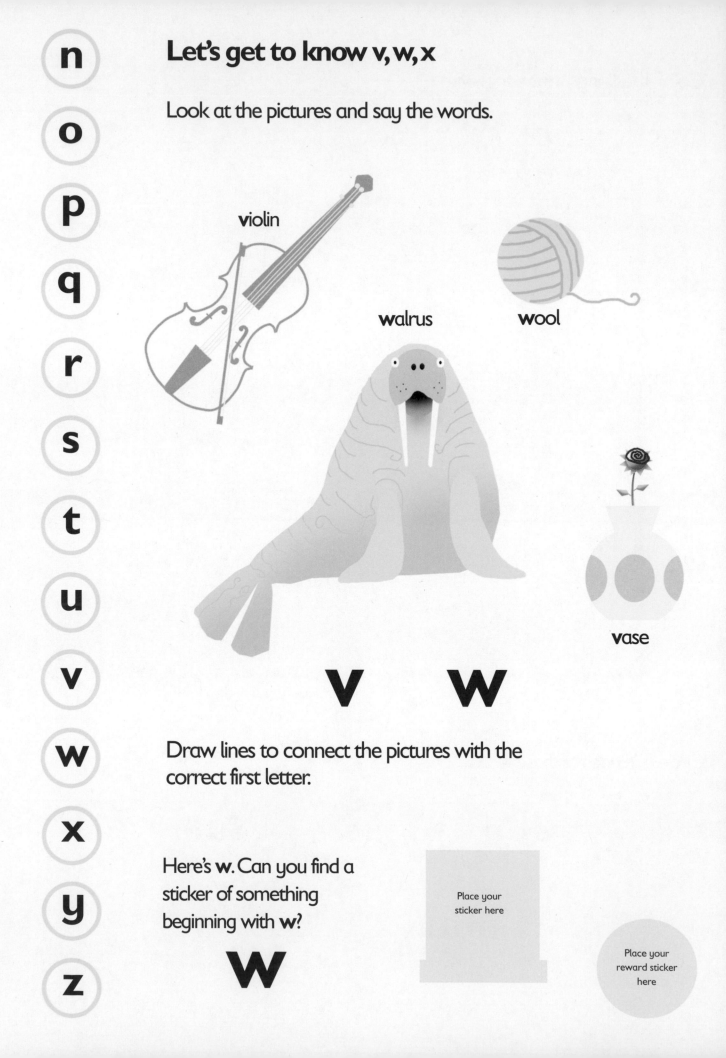

violin

walrus

wool

vase

V   W

Draw lines to connect the pictures with the correct first letter.

Here's **w**. Can you find a sticker of something beginning with **w**?

W

Place your sticker here

Place your reward sticker here

Color the things that begin with **w**.

Circle **x** in each of these words.

fox   box   six

fix   axe

n
o
p
q
r
s
t
u
v
w
x
y
z

Let's get to know y, z

Look at the pictures and say the words.

yo-yo

yacht

zipper

yogurt

zig-zag

y z

Draw lines to connect the pictures with the correct first letter.

a is the first letter in the alphabet.
What is the last?

Color all these yellow things. What are they?

Here's **z**. Can you find a sticker of something beginning with **z**?

z

Place your sticker here

Place your reward sticker here

Do you know other words that begin with **z**?

n o p q r s t u v w x y z

You name it

Can you think of a name for each of these animals? Each name must start with the same letter as the animal. A good name for the parrot would be Peter Parrot.

kangaroo

horse

zebra

monkey

Place your sticker here

panda

Can you find a sticker of Peter Parrot?

Place your reward sticker here

I like ...

Ben and Carl like things that start with the first letter of their names. Draw a line to join Ben and Carl to the thing they like.

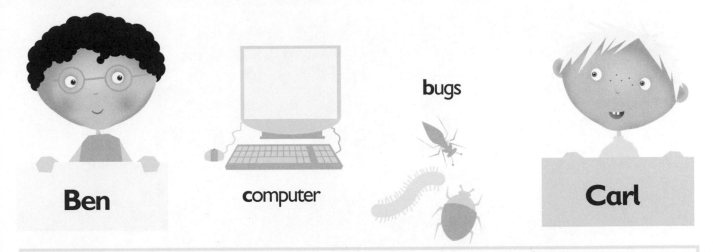

Ben

computer

bugs

Carl

Draw pictures of things that start with the same letter as your name.

Here's Jenny.
Can you find a sticker of something she likes?

Sally

Place your sticker here

Place your reward sticker here

n
o
p
q
r
s
t
u
v
w
x
y
z

P is for party

Paul is having a party! Color the food that begins with **p**.

Can you find a sticker
present for Paul? His
present begins with **p**.
What is it?

Place your
sticker here

Place your
reward sticker
here

It's in your name

Circle the letters that are in your name.

a b c

d e f g h

i j k l m

n o p q r

s t u v w

x y z

Place your reward sticker here

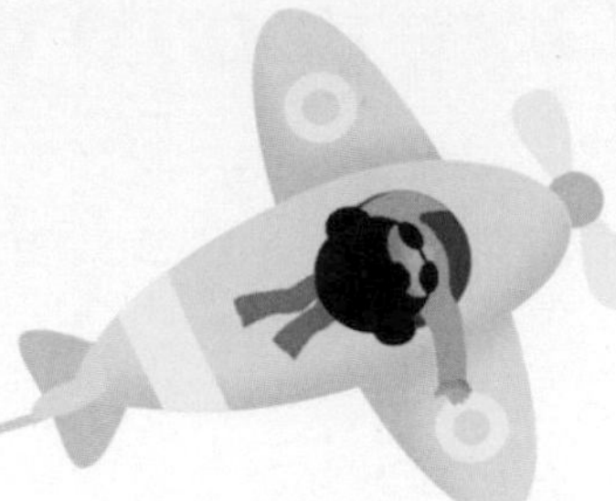

Once upon a time ...

Can you tell the story of Goldilocks and the Three Bears from these pictures?

1.

2.

3.
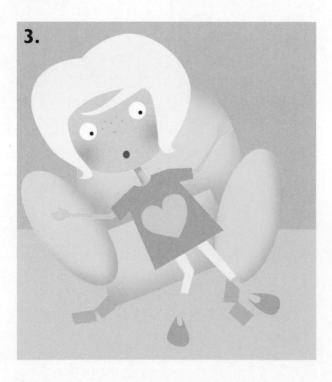

4.

Place your reward sticker here

Tell a story

Look at these four pictures. Can you make
up a story to go with the pictures?

1.

2.

3.

4.

From a to z

Now you know all the letters from **a** to **z**!
Start at **a**, and join the letters in alphabetical order.
What have you drawn?

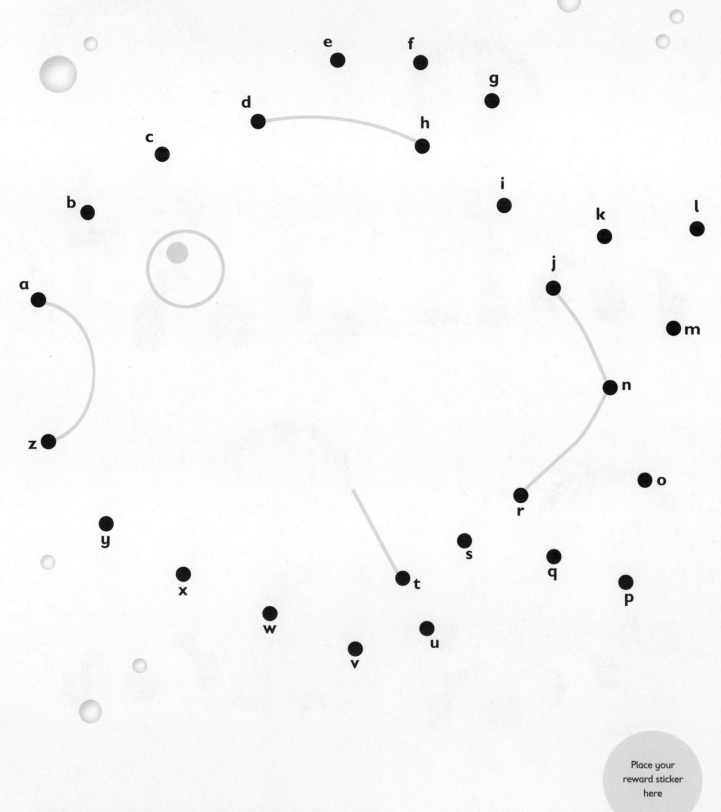

Well done! You're a star for finishing this section.

FIRST TIME LEARNING

READING

AUTUMN
PUBLISHING

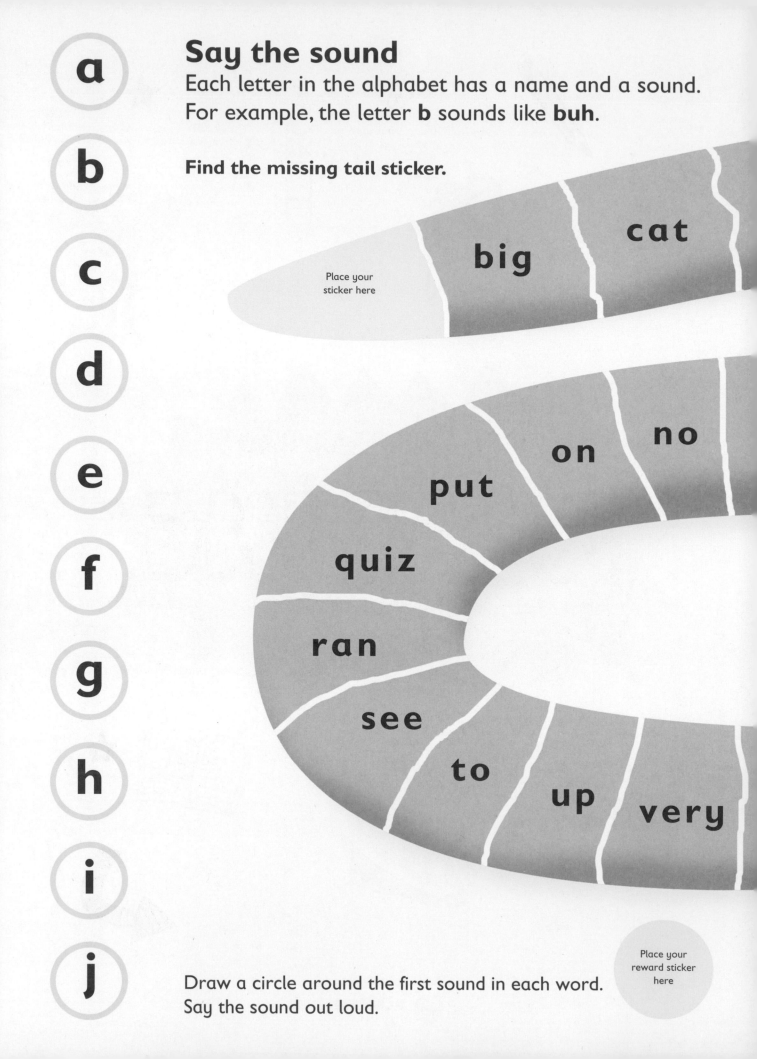

Say the sound

Each letter in the alphabet has a name and a sound.
For example, the letter **b** sounds like **buh**.

Find the missing tail sticker.

a
b
c
d
e
f
g
h
i
j

Place your
sticker here

big

cat

put

on

no

quiz

ran

see

to

up

very

Place your
reward sticker
here

Draw a circle around the first sound in each word.
Say the sound out loud.

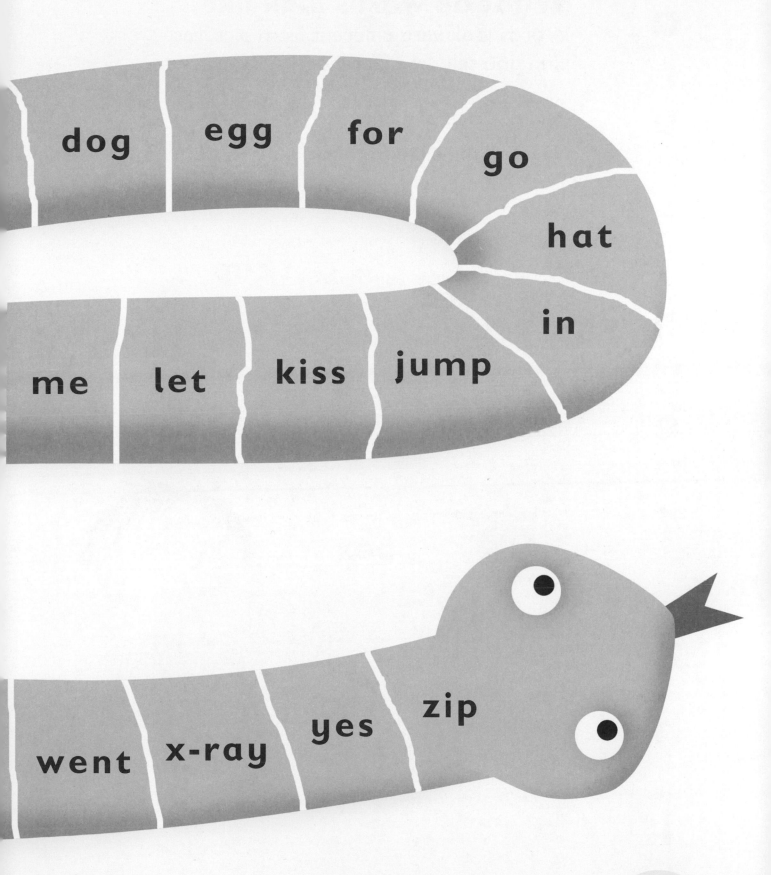

dog egg for go hat

in

me let kiss jump

went x-ray yes zip

Place your reward sticker here

What do words look like?

Words look very different from pictures.
Can you tell the difference?

Find a sticker of a bat.

Now find the bat word sticker.

a
b
c
d
e
f
g
h
i
j

cup

bed

boy

box

rug

Place your sticker here

Place your sticker here

pen

Find the words and circle them.
Point to the pictures.

Place your reward sticker here

Listen to the last sound
Words are made up of many letter sounds.

Ask an adult to say these words. Listen for the sound at the end of each word.
Circle the word that matches the picture.

	sun	sum
	man	mat
	cat	cap
	dog	dot
	six	sit
	pop	pot

The 'a' family

All these words belong to the **a** family because they have an **a** sound in the middle.

Let's say the words. Can you circle the **a** in each word?

a
a
a
a
a
a
a
a

bat

mat

cat

hat

Can you hear the **a** sound?

Sound the first letter of the word, then the **a** sound, then the last letter.

Join the sounds up. Can you say the word?

Find a sticker of a bat in a hat.

Place your sticker here

Place your reward sticker here

More 'a' words

These words belong to the **a** family too, but they have a different sound at the end.

Say the sound of each letter and read the words.
What sound comes at the end of each word?

pan

man

fan

van

Now read these words.

A man ran to the van.

**Find a sticker
of a van.**

Place your
sticker here

Place your
reward sticker
here

The 'e' family

These words are in the **e** family because they have **e** in the middle.

Can you read these words? Circle the **e** in each word.

e
e
e
e
e
e
e
e

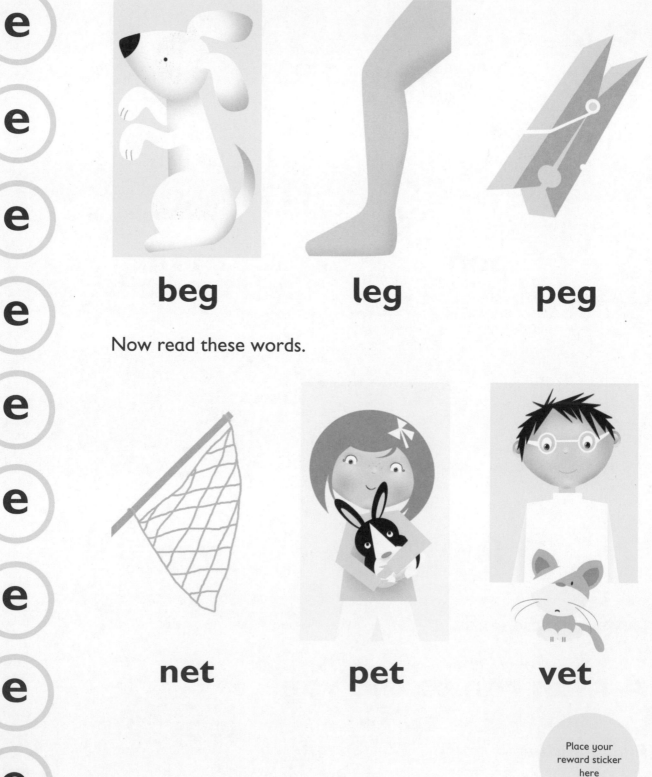

beg　　　**leg**　　　**peg**

Now read these words.

net　　　**pet**　　　**vet**

Place your reward sticker here

More 'e' words

These words have an **e** sound too.

hen

men

pen

ten

Can you read this?

A hen with a pen.

Find a sticker of a hen with a pen.

Place your sticker here

Place your reward sticker here

The 'i' family

There is an **i** sound in all of these words.

Say the words, then circle the **i** in each word.

bin   **fin**   **tin**

What is the last sound in these words?

bib   **nib**   **rib**

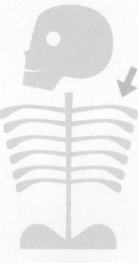

Place your reward sticker here

More i words

These words have an 'i' sound too.
Can you read them all?

pig

dig

big

wig

Can you read this?

A big pig.

Find a sticker of a pig.

Place your
sticker here

Place your
reward sticker
here

The 'o' family

What sound is in the middle of these words?

Circle the middle sound in each word.

cot   **dot**   **pot**

What sound is at the end of these words?
Circle the sound at the end of each word.

hop   **mop**   **top**

Well done!

Place your
reward sticker
here

More 'o' words

Now read these words.

dog

fog

log

jog

Can you read this?

A dog on a log.

Place your sticker here

Place your reward sticker here

Find a sticker of a dog on a log.

The 'u' family

What sound is in the middle of these words?

Circle the middle sound in each word.

u
u
u
u
u
u
u
u

f u n   **s u n**   **r u n**

What sound is at the end of these words?
Circle the sound at the end of each word.

c u t   **h u t**   **n u t**

Place your
reward sticker
here

More 'u' words

Now read these words.

mug

dug

hug

rug

Can you read this?

A bug on a rug.

Find a sticker of a bug.

Place your
sticker here

Place your
reward sticker
here

Now give yourself a **big hug** for reading so well.

Say sh!

Sometimes we join two letters together to make a new sound. We say **sh** for shell.

Can you hear the **sh** sounds in this sentence?

She sells seashells on the seashore.

Draw circles around the **sh** sounds.

sh
sh
sh
sh
sh
sh
sh
sh
sh

Ship starts with **sh**. Can you think of any other **sh** words?

Find a sticker word that begins with sh.
The picture is a clue.

Sh! It's a

Place your sticker here

Place your reward sticker here

I'm glad I'm not a fish!

Sh comes at the end of words too.

Find the missing words on the sticker page.

Read all the words.

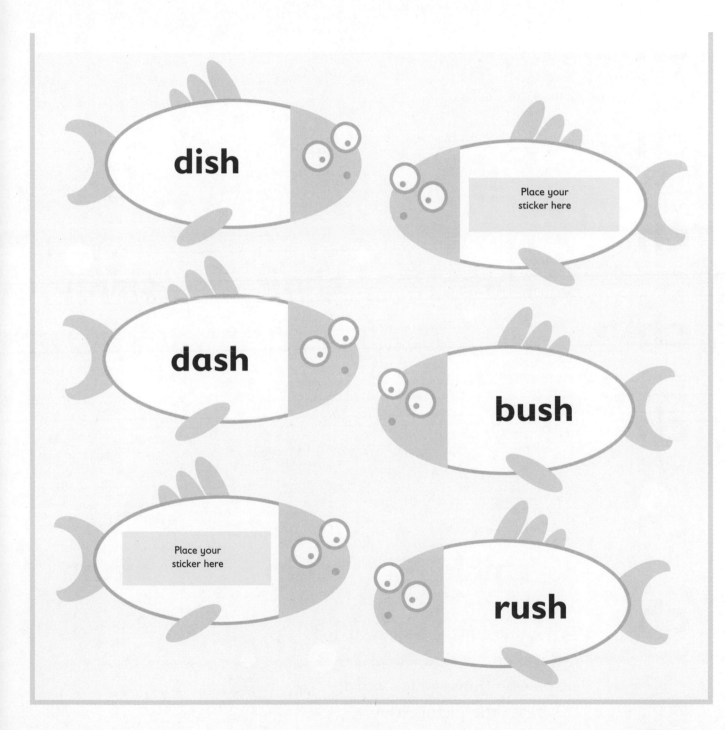

Do you know any more words like these?

Can you make up a word of your own that ends in **sh**?

Ch ch ch!

This is the sound we sometimes make when pretending to be a train chugging out of the station. **Choo-choo!**

Say **ch** at the beginning of these words.

chest

chair

chimp

chick

chin

chain

ch ch ch ch ch ch ch ch ch ch

ch comes at the beginning and at the end of one word! Can you guess which word? Look at the picture clue. **Find the word sticker.**

Place your sticker here

Place your reward sticker here

Th ...

We sometimes say **th** at the beginning of words.

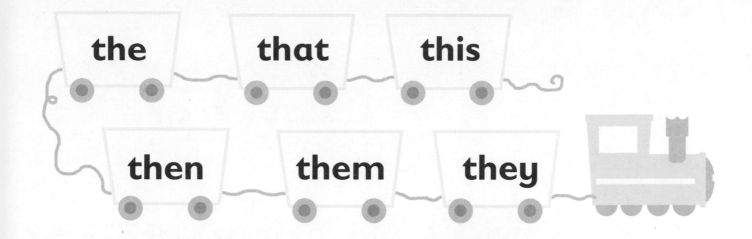

Can you think of any more **th** words? Write them here.

… …
… …

Write **th** words in this rhyme to finish it.

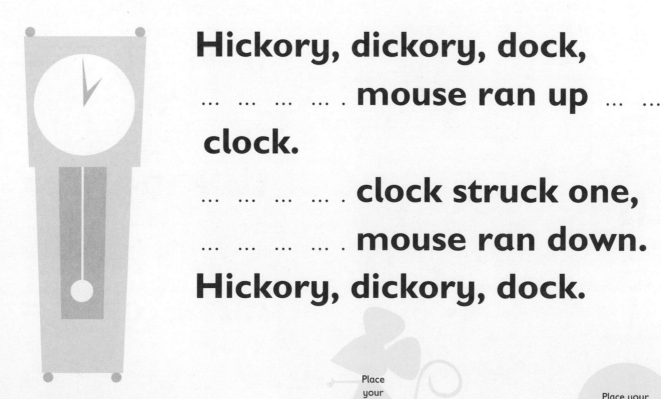

Hickory, dickory, dock,
… … … … . **mouse ran up** … …
clock.
… … … … . **clock struck one,**
… … … … . **mouse ran down.**
Hickory, dickory, dock.

Place your sticker here

Place your reward sticker here

Find a sticker of a mouse.

Beginnings and endings

Here are some more words!

Join the letter sounds together and say the words.

a b c d e f g h i j

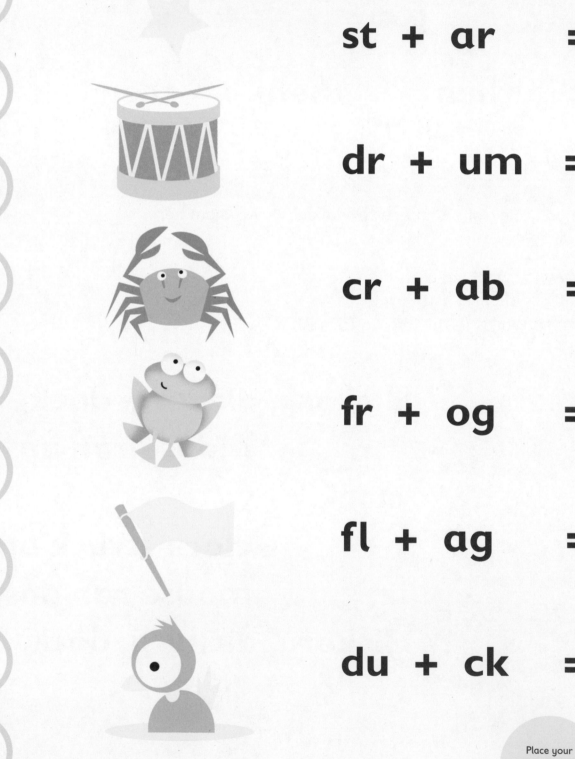

st + ar =

dr + um =

cr + ab =

fr + og =

fl + ag =

du + ck =

Words with ee

Read the words and point to the pictures.

three   **tree**   **feet**   **knee**

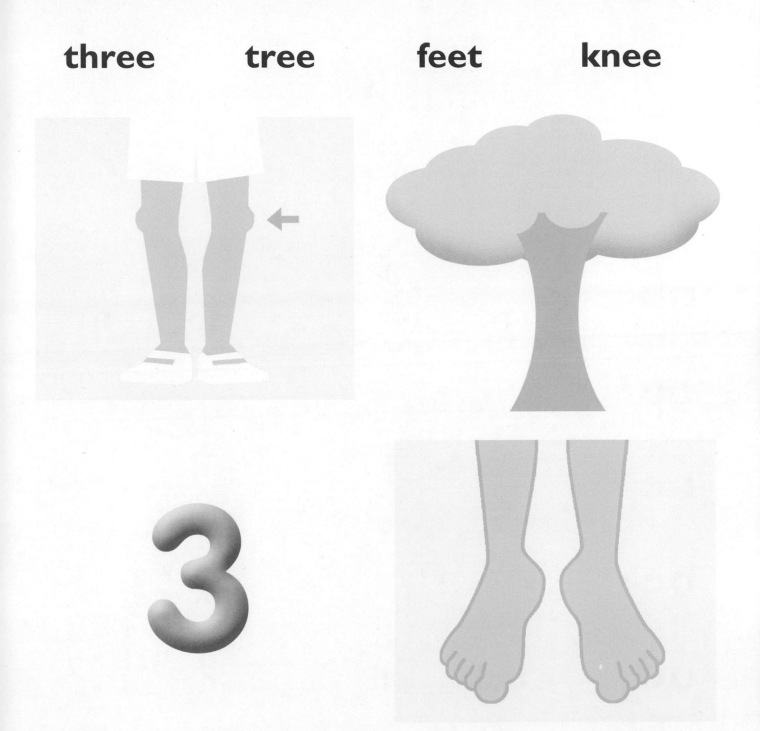

Draw lines from the pictures to the words.

Do you know any other **ee** words?

Find a sticker of a bee.

Place your sticker here

Place your reward sticker here

OO! Look at you!

Look at these pictures and say the **oo** words.
Write **oo** to complete the words.

OO

oo

oo

oo

oo

oo

oo

oo

oo

oo

m ___ n

sp ___ n

ball ___ n

r ___ m

Who ran away with a
spoon in a famous nursery
rhyme? Who jumped over
the **moon**?

Find the sticker.

Place your
sticker here

Place your
reward sticker
here

Ends with st

Read the words and point to the pictures.
Draw lines to join the pictures to the words.

nest **chest** **first** **vest**

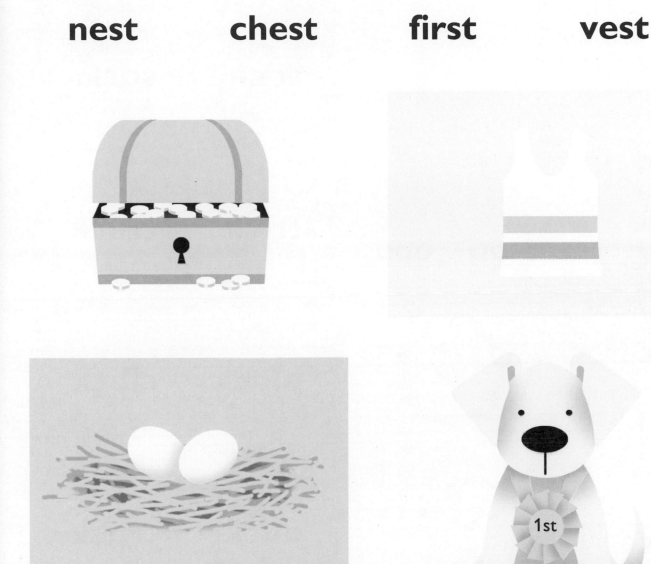

Here are some more **st** words.
Can you read them?

best **last** **test**

west **zest**

You are the **best** at reading!

Circle ck

Circle the word that matches the picture.

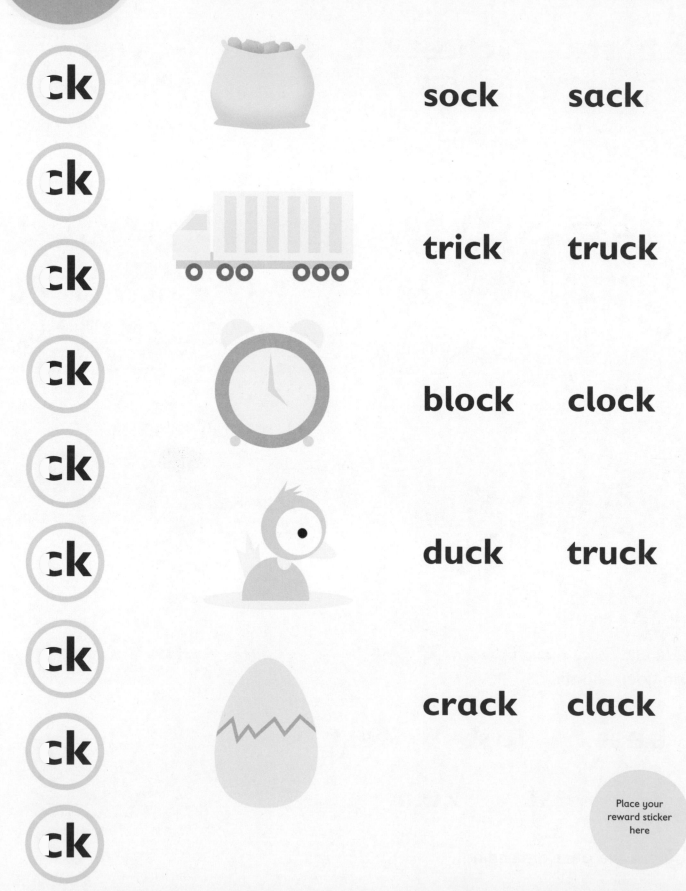

sock   sack

trick   truck

block   clock

duck   truck

crack   clack

Rhyming sounds

Listen for the sounds at the end of these words.

lock   **sock**   **rock**

When words end in the same sound they rhyme.
What sounds do these words have in common?

Find a word sticker that ends with the sound **...ock**.

Here's a clue, just for you.

Tick, tock goes the
Place your
sticker here

Place your
reward sticker
here

f

g h i j k l m n o

Huff and puff!

Circle the words that match the pictures.

cuff   huff   puff   muff

"I'll huff and I'll puff and
I'll blow your house down!"

Place
your
sticker
here

Who said this?

Place your
reward sticker
here

Find the picture sticker to show the answer.

Color the rhyme

Say the words out loud, then color the things that rhyme in each line.

hen

cup

pen

pip

bed

zip

mop

hop

box

skip

ship

shop

You're a **star**. You'll go **far**!

Time for a rhyme

r

Find the sticker rhyming words to finish these rhymes.

s
t
u
v
w
x
y
z

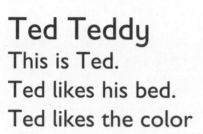

Ted Teddy
This is Ted.
Ted likes his bed.
Ted likes the color

> Place your sticker here

Molly Dolly
This is Molly.
Molly is a dolly.
Molly's friend is

> Place your sticker here

> Place your reward sticker here

Pat the Rat
This is Pat.
Pat is a rat.
Pat doesn't like the

Place your sticker here

Lin and Min
This is Lin.
Lin's twin is called Min.
Min has a fish, and he is called

Place your sticker here

Place your reward sticker here

m

n
o
p
q
r
s
t
u
v

Three little monkeys

Let's say the rhyme out loud!

Listen for the sound at the end of the last word in each line.

Three little monkeys jumping on the bed,
One fell off and bumped its head.
Mummy phoned the doctor,
And the doctor said,
"No more jumping on the bed!"

Find the words in the poem that rhyme.

Did you find them all?

Place your
reward sticker
here

bed   head   said

Tired teddy bear

Can you work out the missing words in the teddy bear rhyme?

Teddy bear, teddy bear,
Climb the _____ .

Teddy bear, teddy bear,
Say your _____ .

Teddy bear, teddy bear,
Turn off the light.

Teddy bear, teddy bear,
Say "Goodnight!"

Now you can make rhyming words!

Twinkle twinkle

Where have all the rhyming words gone?

Can you say the rhyme and add the missing words?

Twinkle, twinkle, little _____ ,

How I wonder what you _____ .

Up above the world so _____ ,

Like a diamond in the _____ .

Twinkle, twinkle, little _____ ,

How I wonder what you _____ .

Place your reward sticker here

Well done! You are a little star for finishing this section.

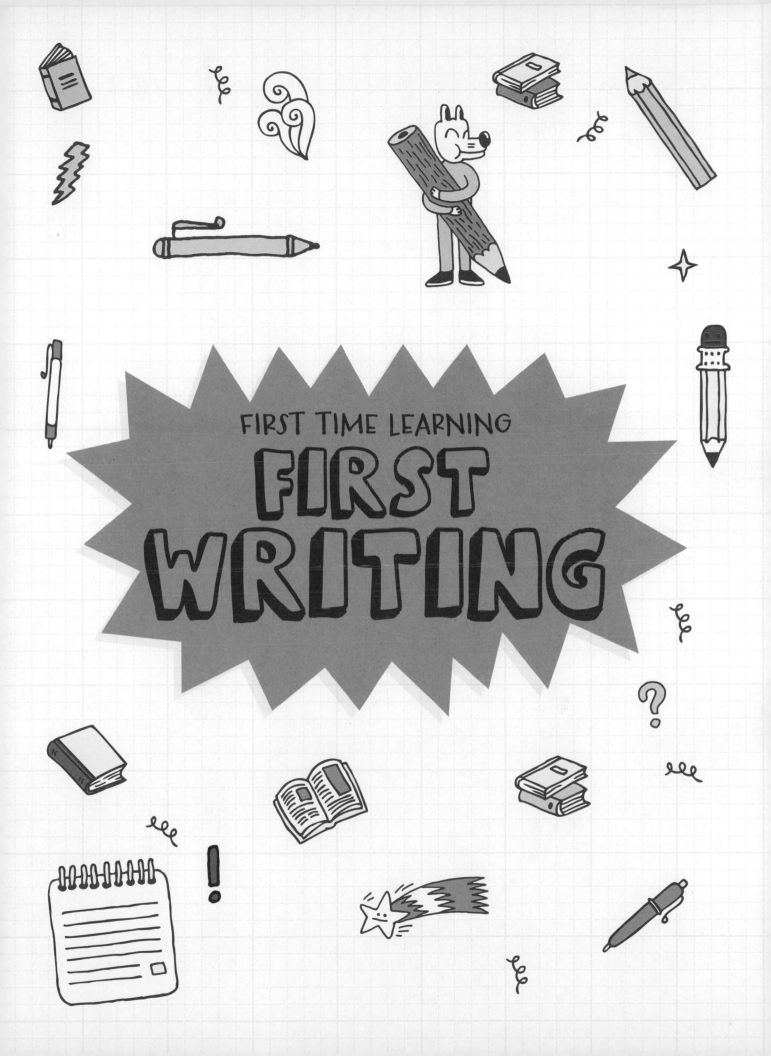

FIRST TIME LEARNING

FIRST WRITING

On target!

Remember two things when you are learning to write:
1. Hold your pencil lightly, not tightly!
2. Go from left to right across the page.

From here • • • • • • • • • • • • • • to here.
Follow the line with your pencil to reach the target.

Place your sticker here

Find a sticker of an apple on a log.

Place your reward sticker here

Going down!

Let's go down the page now.

Trace the arrows.

Seeing stripes

Trace the stripes to make everything in this picture stripy!

Place your sticker here

Place your reward sticker here

Find a stripy bug sticker.

Flower power!
Draw lines from the flowers to the pots to finish the pictures. Color in the flowers.

Place your
sticker here

Find a flowerpot sticker.

Place your
reward sticker
here

Amazing maze!

Find a 'way out' sticker for the maze.

Now draw a line to take you through the maze to the way out.

Place your
sticker here

Place your
reward sticker
here

Curly whirlies!

Trace the curly lines going down the page.
Keep your pencil on the paper until you reach
the end.

Place your
sticker here

Place your
reward sticker
here

When you reach the bottom,
find the missing skier sticker.

Twisty turns!

When we write, we make lots of twisty turns on the page.
Trace the twisty turns from left to right with your pencil.

Place your
sticker here

When you reach the end,

find the missing plane sticker.

Place your
reward sticker
here

Let's go around

Let's learn to draw a circle.

Start at the top and follow the dotted line around.

Don't take your pencil off the page.

A circle is like the letter **o**.

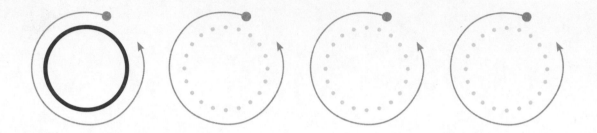

Circle it

Trace the lines to draw around these circle shapes.

Can you find the missing clock face on the sticker page?

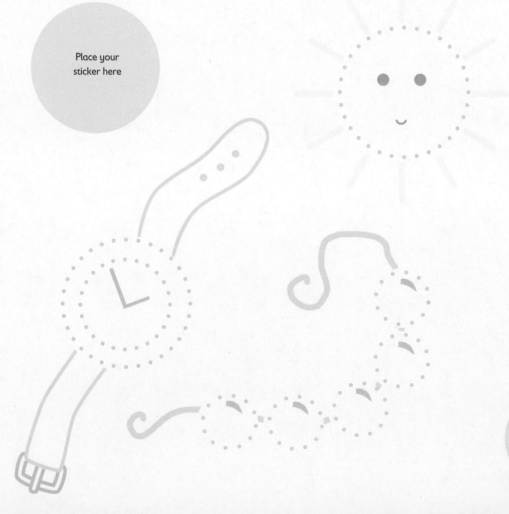

Place your
sticker here

Place your
reward sticker
here

Part of a circle

Look what happens if we stop on the way around.
It looks just like the letter **c**.
Try it for yourself.

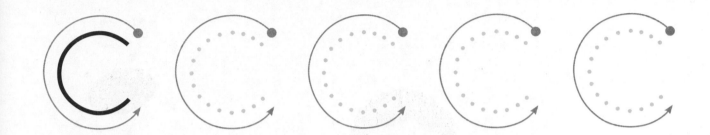

Trace the c

Trace the **c** shapes in these pictures.

Place your
reward sticker
here

Perfect pets

Anna has stripy pets and Tim has pets that are spotted.
Finish the pictures of Anna's and Tim's pets by tracing
the straight lines and circles.

Rolo robot

Trace the dotted lines
to finish the robot.

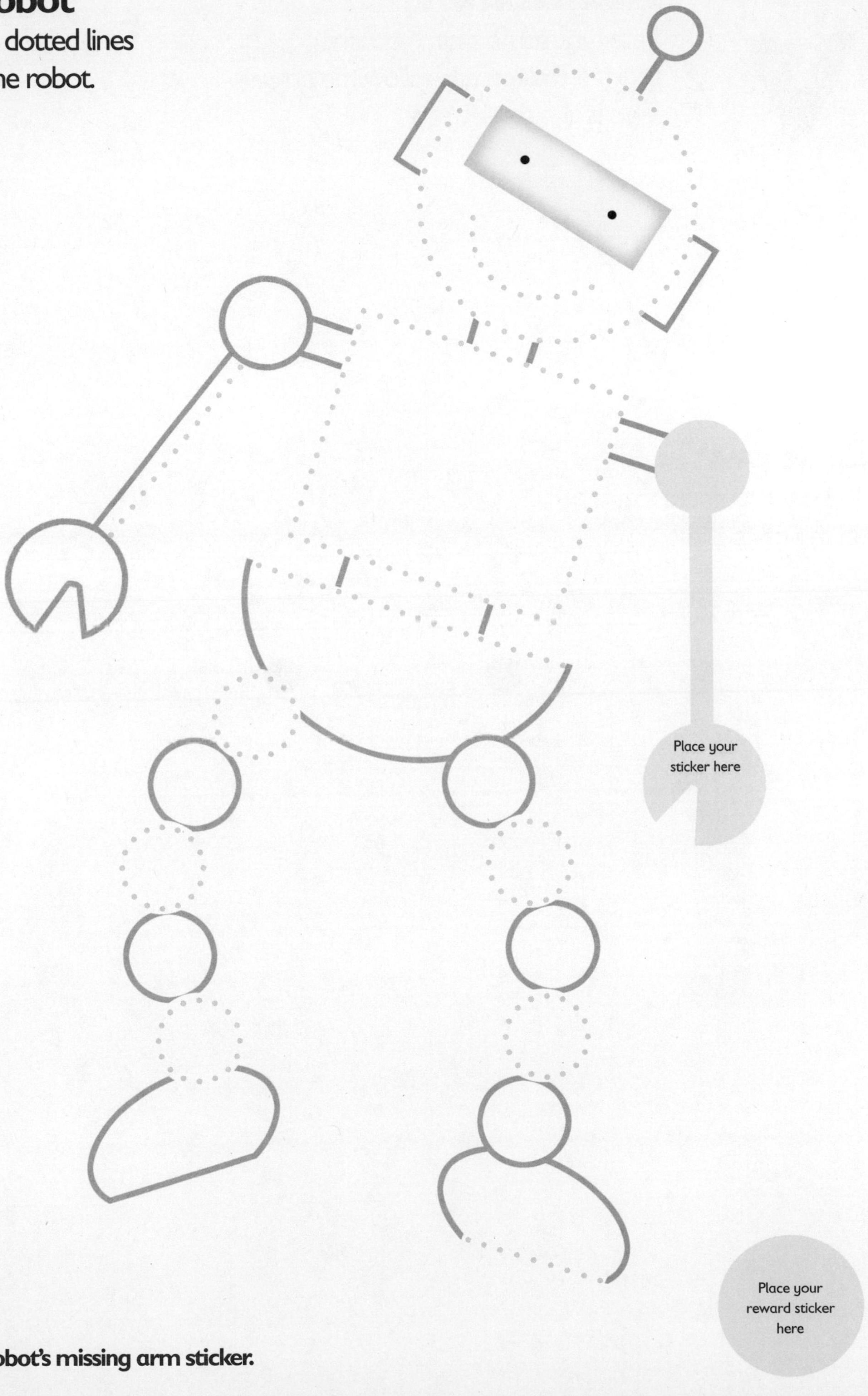

Place your
sticker here

Place your
reward sticker
here

Find the robot's missing arm sticker.

Sharp corners

Let's turn some sharp corners!
Start at the top and follow the arrows.
This is like the letter **v**.

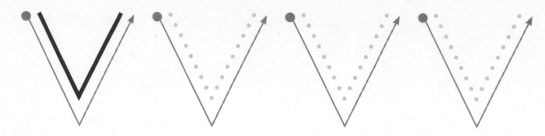

Little owl

Trace the feathers
on the owl's chest.

Lost in the snow

Draw a line following the arrows to escape from the snow monster.

Place your sticker here

Place your reward sticker here

Find the snow monster's hat sticker.

Crossing over

Let's make some lines cross over.
Trace the dotted lines, following the arrows.
This is how we write the letter **x**.

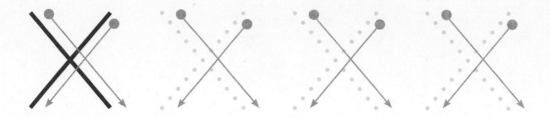

Clowning about

Trace the **X**s to finish the picture.

Place your sticker here

Place your reward sticker here

Find a ball

sticker.

Treasure hunt

X marks the spot where the treasure is hidden.
Draw a line through this maze to the letter **x**.

Place your
sticker here

X

Now find your treasure on the sticker page.

Place your
reward sticker
here

Big and little

Let's try some writing patterns.
Trace each pattern and draw more to finish each row.

Find a sticker of a little caterpillar.

Can you make the big caterpillar look like the little one?

Place your sticker here

Place your reward sticker here

Snowflakes

Draw more snowflakes like these.
Draw some different ones of your own, too!

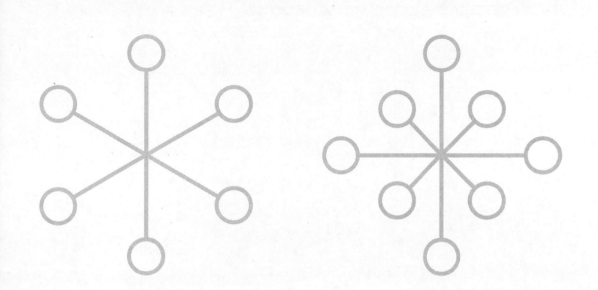

Place your
sticker here

Place your
reward sticker
here

Find a snowman sticker.

Loop the loops

Can you draw loops?
A loop goes up and back and crosses over.
Make a big loop in the air with your arm.
Now trace these loops with your pencil.

Lovely loops!

Find a sticker of a kite.
Draw a looped string for the kite.

Place your
sticker here

Place your
reward sticker
here

Animal tracks

Trace the animal tracks. Stay on the lines.
Go from left to right.

Find a spider sticker.

Now finish the spider's web.

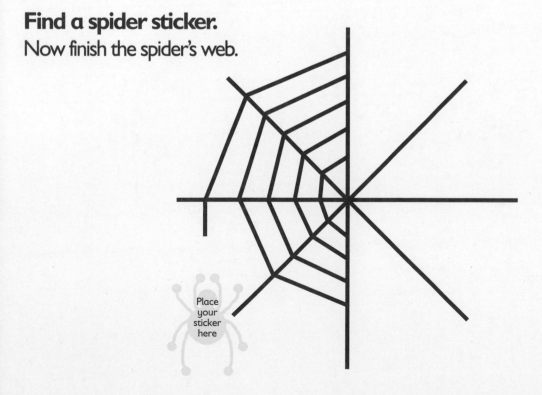

Place
your
sticker
here

Place your
reward sticker
here

Bend it!

It starts like a letter **c**, but then bends the other way. It's the letter **s**!

Start at the top and trace the dotted line, following the arrows. Don't take your pencil off the page.

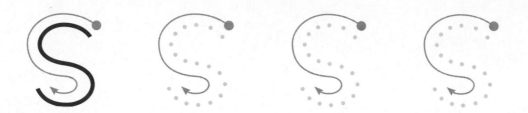

Under the sea

Find an eel sticker.

How many **s** shapes can you find in this sea picture?

Place your sticker here

Place your reward sticker here

Racetrack

Follow the bends in the tracks with your pencil to win the race!
Start at the top and keep inside the lines.

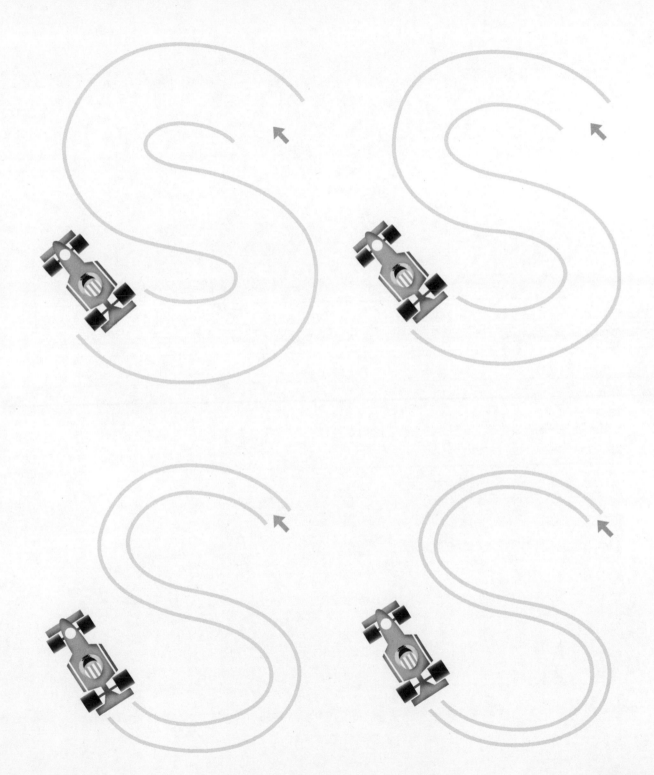

Which car was best and didn't go over the lines?

Follow the leader
Trace the tracks with your pencil.
Find the missing picture sticker.

Jump like the squirrel.

Ride the waves.

Place your
sticker here

Bounce on the pogo stick.

Place your
reward sticker
here

Keep on track!

Try to keep your pencil on the page until you finish the line.

Climb the mountains.

Walk along the castle wall.

Race along the track.

Circus act

Trace the lines to finish the picture.

Place your sticker here

Find a sticker of a juggler's baton.

Now color the picture.

Shape it

Now you know lots of the shapes we use for writing.
Complete this picture using all the shapes you know.

Place your sticker here

Place your reward sticker here

Find a present sticker.

Super spirals
Try drawing a spiral!

Draw one in the air with your finger first.
Start in the middle and go around and
around and around …
Now trace the line to draw a spiral with your pencil.
Find the planet sticker.

Place your
sticker here

START

Place your
reward sticker
here

Zany zigzags

You've drawn zigzags going across, now let's draw zigzags going down as well!

Can you spot the letter **w** or the letter **z** in any of these zigzags?

Writing words

Follow the dotted lines to write these words.
Then draw the pictures.

Find a cup sticker.

man

cup

hat

Place your
sticker here

Place your
reward sticker
here

Face shapes

Can you draw a picture of your face using shapes?

Draw one large circle for your head.

Now draw two small circles for eyes.

A pointy shape for a nose.

Then half a circle for a mouth.

Draw some wavy or straight lines for hair.

NAME . . . .

Now color your picture carefully.

Can you write your name under your face?

Writing more words

Follow the dotted lines to write the words.
Then draw the pictures.

Find a sticker of the sun.

sun

owl

cat

Place your
sticker here

Place your
reward sticker
here

Sunny street
Write these words to label the picture.

sun

roof

van

tree

Now color in the picture.

And finally ...
You've done it! You've finished the book.
Can you write the happy words below?

I did it!

Yes!

Yippee!

Hooray!

Well done! You're a star for finishing this book!